KT-130-579

PRAYING IT HOW IT IS AS A TEENAGE GIRL

SHARON JACKSON

WINCHESTER SCHOOL OF MISSION

06042

Kevin
Mayhew

First published in 1996 by
KEVIN MAYHEW LTD
Rattlesden
Bury St Edmunds
Suffolk IP30 0SZ

© 1996 Kevin Mayhew Limited

The right of Sharon Jackson to be identified as the
author of this work has been asserted by her
in accordance with the Copyright, Designs
and Patents Act 1988.

All rights reserved. No part of this publication may
be reproduced, stored in a retrieval system, or
transmitted, in any form or by any means, electronic,
mechanical, photocopying, recording or otherwise,
without the prior written permission of the publisher.

Scripture quotations taken from the *Holy Bible,
New International Version.*
Copyright © 1973, 1978, 1984 by *International
Bible Society*. Used by permission of Hodder &
Stoughton Limited. All rights reserved.
'NIV' is a registered trademark of
International Bible Society.
UK trademark number 1448790

0 1 2 3 4 5 6 7 8 9

ISBN 086209 925 0
Catalogue No 1500085

Front cover by Jeff Parker
Edited by David Gatward
Typesetting by Louise Hill
Printed and bound in Great Britain

*For Mum, Dad, brother Grant
and boyfriend Mark.*

I love you all.

CONTENTS

ACKNOWLEDGEMENTS

I would like to say a big thank you to all the people who have played a big part in my life and who have not only inspired and influenced the prayers in this book but who have also inspired and influenced me as a person. Special thanks go to:

(Cast in order of appearance!)

Mum, Dad and Grant: For all your love, support and guidance (and for just putting up with me!) The greatest family anyone could hope to have!

Grandma, Granddad and Uncle Geoff: For taking me to church with you when I was a little girl and helping to sow those first seeds, and, of course, for all your love.

Keith Topham: For offering me a doorway into the Church and a new faith, and for all the fun productions you gave me the opportunity to be part of.

'Rockin Rev' Gordon Gatward: For all your many words of wisdom and for all the sunshine you bring into people's lives. (Special thanks for the rock climbing, abseiling, canoeing, archery, etc., etc.)

Stage II: For always reminding me that being a Christian can be fun, with, of course, special thanks to **Vicky 'the Vixen' Lawson** (thanks for all those late night chats/ giggling sessions) and **Cathy 'the match maker' Charlesworth** (thanks for all those mad parties). I would also like to say a big 'miss you' to **John 'the clown' Gatward** and **Dave 'the editor' Gatward** (thanks for remembering me, Dave!)

Wesley Memorial Church: Too many wonderful people to mention by name but you know who you are. Special thanks though to **Sister Mary** for inspiring my interest in third world issues – I'll get there eventually.

'Rev Ev' David Evans: For all those dinner time chats and excellent barbecues (even if most of them ended up indoors!)

The Lads: What can I say, boys? Thanks for my honorary membership and 'Howay the lads!'

All my friends from Trinity and All Saints: For three excellent years, with special thanks to **Chaley 'Mad McMad' Thompson, Peter '007' Jarmain** and **Clare 'Storyteller/ Showsinger' Felton** – my college family. I promise to stay in touch. (PS. remember downtown L.A.?)

Mark Gargett: Last but by no means least, the most patient and caring boyfriend in the world. I love you!

INTRODUCTION

Why roller coaster? Well a friend once referred to me as an emotional roller coaster (you will probably see what she means when you read my prayers!) and, as I see it, even the most stable of people cannot live through the teenage years without encountering a fair variety of ups and downs. So, having chosen to write about those many ups and downs I really could not think of a better title.

So, hello and welcome on board, I hope you enjoy the ride.

These prayers were not difficult to write, basically because they are simply an amalgamation of many prayers that I have said to God throughout my teenage years. It was, however, fairly difficult to put them forward for publishing. Why? Well, because baring your heart and soul on paper is one thing, but knowing that other people may be reading what you have got to say is entirely different. Anyway, if you are reading this now then that pretty much means that I no longer have any secrets. (Aaaaarrrggh!)

To be honest this book is really just a long-winded way of saying to other teenagers, girls in particular, 'I've been there and know how you are feeling. You are not alone.' In this way I hope I am able to offer a little comfort and hope to anyone who is going through any of the things I have been through. It is also a big thank you to God for all he has done for me and for bringing me through all this in one piece (and almost completely sane!)

Anyway, I'll stop rambling on about the book and let you read it for yourself. I hope you get as much out of reading it as I got out of writing it.

Cheerio and God bless.

Sharon

SEARCHING

I look around me, Lord,
    and all I see is people
    forever searching,
    exploring,
    experimenting,
    challenging.

Trying to discover the undiscovered,
    trying to explain the unexplained,
    trying to attain the unattained.
And why, Lord?

Well I'm not too sure to be honest,
    and I doubt that even they know
    for certain.
But I suppose they are all in search
    of some kind of fulfilment,
    some form of contentment,
    or happiness,
    or inner self-assurance.

So, sportsmen and women
    strive for record-breaking performances,
    scientists seek the answers
    to the world's many riddles,
    business managers aim to maximise their
    returns and profit margins,

and teenagers experiment with drugs,
alcohol and sex.

Still others turn to various
    religious experiences for inspiration,
    whilst some take more of an interest in
    the material aspects of life
    and invest their hopes
    in the weekly lottery draw.

The means are not important, Lord,
    but one thing is clear,
    we are all searching for something,
    and it's hardly surprising is it?

I mean, we live in a world
    where so-called rational thought is
    the religion of the day.
Where work, for many,
    offers no other reward
    than the pay packet which is received
    at the end of each week.
Where community spirit and charity
    have made way for a
    'survival of the fittest' philosophy.

And the result?
A world full of people
    who see no meaning in life,
    no point to their existence.

A world where everybody
   is constantly searching
   for something,
   but nobody is quite sure what.
A world full of people
   trying almost anything
   to fill the emptiness they feel,
   to find some sense
   of fulfilment.

And they may find it, Lord.
The athlete may be content
   with a gold medal.
The business manager may be satisfied
   with an increase in sales.
But for how long?
Surely their fulfilment
   will only be temporary.

The problem is, Lord,
   that everybody is searching,
   and they are all searching
   for the wrong thing.
They should be searching for you, Lord,

I have come to realise, Lord,
   through my few years
   of searching for that something,
   that it is only by entering
   into a relationship with you

that true fulfilment can be found.
True contentment,
    true happiness,
    true self-assurance.

And it does not come from having made
    any earth-shattering discovery
    or revelation.
It does not come from achieving anything
    out of the ordinary.
It does not come from challenging anything
    or anyone.
It comes simply from knowing you, Lord.

It comes from knowing
    that I am loved
    by you.

Lord,
    I just want to pray
    for all those searching souls out there
    who continue their quest
    unaware of the simple truth.
I pray that they may come to realise
    that fulfilment is well within their reach.
If only they would hold out their hands
    and welcome you into their lives.

That doesn't mean that they will ever stop
    striving to attain ambitious goals,

I know that, Lord.
But it does mean
    that they can experience
    that inner peace that comes
    from knowing you,
    and maybe
    stop their vain searching.

Amen.

*He who has the Son has life; he who does
not have the Son of God does not have life.*

1 John 5:12

WHAT ARE YOU TO ME?

What are you to me, Lord?
What are you to me?

Well, you are my father and my mother,
    all rolled into one.
      encouraging me when the going gets
        tough,
      chastising me when I do wrong,
      but the one who always loves me,
      regardless.

You are my teacher and my guide,
    helping me to learn right from wrong,
    pointing me towards the directions
    I should take,
    then fighting tirelessly
    to keep me on course.
My ever-watchful shepherd.

You are my companion and my confidante,
    knowing my fears and my doubts,
    participating in my hopes and my dreams,
    sharing every aspect
    of my life.
My eternal friend.

You are my counsellor and my social worker,
    cheering me when I am sad,
    assuring me when I am anxious,
    comforting me when I despair.
My inner peace.

You are my strength and my security,
    holding me up when I am unable
    to support myself,
    fighting for me long after
    I have given up,
    protecting me from life's many blows.
My steadfast shield.

You are my saviour and my hope,
    showing me the light in a dark world,
    saving me from myself,
    delivering me from my own sin.
The only one who would die for me.

You are everything to me, Lord,
Everything I could ever want or need.

I know, Lord,
    that I am not worthy of all you do for me,
    of all you give to me,
    of all you are to me.

But I also know
    that you are a merciful
    and wonderful God.

That all you have offered me
    has been borne out of your awesome love
      for me,
    and for that I am eternally grateful.

So, Lord,
    I want to thank you and praise you,
    I want to exalt your holy name,
    I want to glorify
    your magnificent kingdom.

For I know what you are to me, God,
    you are my Lord,
    and I pray that this will always be so,
    because without you I have nothing,
    I am nothing.

Amen.

I love you, O Lord, my strength.
The Lord is my rock, my fortress
and my deliverer;
my God is my rock, in whom I take refuge.
He is my shield and the horn of my
salvation, my stronghold.

Psalms 18:1, 2

WE ARE FAMILY

My mum.
How can I sum up my mum?
Well she is certainly gregarious.
Within weeks of introducing her
    to new friends, I find myself questioning
    who they are calling around to see,
    me or her?
And she is very good at mothering as well,
    especially when it comes to food, Lord.
I'm sure you've heard of compulsive eaters.
Well allow me to introduce my mum,
    the world's first-ever compulsive feeder.
But she's not all soft-hearted,
    cuddly mum, you know.
Oh no!
She is rather astute as well.
In fact, Lord,
    she adds a whole new dimension
    to the phrase, 'Mum always knows best'.
With my mum it's a case of, 'Mum always
    knows best and has told everyone else
    what best is long before anyone else has
    even had a bash at guessing'.
Something which can be very annoying
    for someone trying very hard
    to be a rebellious teenager,
    especially when you have to keep

    admitting
that she was right all along.

Then there's my dad,
How can I sum up my dad?
Well, as he likes to remind us all
    frequently, a more easy-going,
    kind-natured man
    you couldn't hope to meet.
The thing is, it's probably true.
He's also the biggest kid in the world.
One thing's for sure – if being childlike
    guarantees entry to heaven then he's going
    to be at the front of the queue,
    with his terrible jokes and pranks,
    his great passion for toys and cartoons,
    his great ability to be one of the lads,
    and that cheeky grin that sneaks across
    his face when he is desperately trying
    to keep it straight.
Perhaps unbelievably,
    he's also very wise.
Not just academically clever,
    although he certainly is that.
But also in a godly sense,
    forever helping me and so many others
    to develop new and exciting depths
    to our faith.

Then there's my brother.
How can I sum up my brother?
Well, in two parts I would say.
There is Grant as everyone gets to see him,
    the party animal,
    wacky and mad
    and really great fun.
Always thinking up some bizarre scheme,
    whether it is growing his hair
    down beyond his shoulders
    and then getting it all
    completely shaved off,
    or maybe just finding out how loud
    he can actually play his stereo and guitar
    simultaneously without Mum and Dad
    throwing him out of the house.

Then there's the side
    that only a privileged few
    ever get to see.
The thoughtful and quiet Grant,
    the very bright and good-looking bloke
    who is actually rather under-confident
    and insecure about himself.
The caring and affectionate brother and son.

And there's my grandparents
    and uncle as well, Lord.
How can I sum them up?
Well, they are the three most generous people

anyone could ever meet.
They give so much and yet they will accept
    so little in return.
And sometimes it can be so frustrating
    to know that all they give,
    all they do,
    and all they are for others
    can never be repaid.
And their passion for life cannot fail
    to inspire, Lord.
All that seemingly boundless energy
    they invest in making the most
    of every day,
    with their dancing,
    their gardening,
    their travelling,
    their love of music,
    and their steadfast faith.

So what do these people
    all have in common, Lord?
Well, they are my family of course
My loving, supportive and caring family.
They all mean so much to me, Lord.
I love all of them so very much,
    and I really just want to thank you
    for them all.
I know we have had disagreements in the
    past,
    I don't know a family who hasn't,

but when it comes down to it, Lord,
we have come through a lot together.

We have been there for each other,
    overcoming our internal differences
    so we can stand as a team
    against the evil and pain
    of this world.

Lord, it is often said that you can choose
    your friends but you cannot choose
    your family.
The thing is,
    if I could choose my family
    I would definitely choose the family
    I have now,
    warts and all!
Because not only are they my family
    but they are my friends and allies.

So thank you, Lord.
Thank you that I was born
    into such a wonderful family.
Help them all to realise
    how special they are,
    how much I love them,
    and how grateful I am to them all.

And please, Lord,
    help all those

who are not as fortunate
as I am.

Those who have lost loved ones,
    those whose family
    has been painfully divided,
    those who have never really known
    family life in the way that I have.

I can't ever pretend to know how they feel,
    or understand their situation,
    but I do pray for them.

Because families can be great, Lord,
    and I'm sure that mine
    must be one of the greatest.

Amen.

CRUMBLING FOUNDATIONS

Oh, Lord, I sit here now in total numbness
   and shock,
I don't know what to think,
   I don't know how to feel,
   I don't know what to say.
All I do know, Lord, is that I need to pray.
That I need to feel your comforting presence.

You see, Lord,
   all my life I have made mistakes,
   made the wrong decisions,
   said the wrong things.
From the day I took my first few steps
   and fell flat on my bum,
   to yesterday when,
   roller-blading down a hill,
   I skated straight into my friend.

And of course there have been far more
   serious mistakes than these.
Going out with the wrong boys,
   choosing the wrong friends,
   not working hard enough in my A-levels.
I'm sure I don't need to continue.

The thing is, Lord,
   no matter how stupid I have been,

no matter how many times,
there have always been two people
who have picked me up,
brushed me down
and helped me try again.

There has always been a shoulder to cry on,
    a wise head to give me advice.
Basically, Lord,
    my foundations have always been strong.
They have always held me up,
    supported me throughout.

I am of course
    talking about my parents, Lord,
    Mum and Dad.
Those two people who have provided
    the advice, care, help
    and unconditional love
    upon which I have built my life.

The problem is, Lord, that, well,
    my parents have just always been there
    when I needed them.
They always seemed so infallible,
    unshakeable,
    even perhaps . . .
    immortal?

And now, Lord,

I feel the foundations crumble
   beneath my feet,
I feel the walls shattering around me.
All of a sudden, Lord,
   the immortal has become very mortal,
The infallible, very fallible.

And I am too scared to even allow myself
   to consider what would happen
   if I did lose my mum.
It all seems far too unreal,
   like this must be someone else's life
   I am hearing about.
The thing is, Lord, I know it's mine.

And I'm just so scared, Lord.
For my mum,
   for the rest of my family,
   for me.

What can I say and do to help anyone,
   to help even myself?
How can any of us deal with this?
How can any of us remain standing
   when our worlds are falling apart?

So, Lord, all I can do is pray.
Pray for my mum.
That you will help her to deal with all the
   thoughts and fears that are going through

her head at the moment,
That you will help her to cope
   with all that she must now face;
   all the treatment,
   all the decisions,
   all the pain and discomfort.

Lord, I also pray for my family,
   that you will comfort them
   and support them,
   that you will help them to cope with
   their fear and grief.

And I pray for myself, Lord.
Please help me to cope.
Help me to put aside my own fears and grief
   so that I can give back just a little of
   the support that my parents have given
   me over the years.
Lord, help me to be optimistic and hopeful.
Help me to be there when I am needed.
Help me to hold up
   the crumbling foundations of our lives
   so that we may all remain strong
   throughout this ordeal.

Amen.

DEATH IS NOTHING

Death is nothing?

That's what the poem said, Lord.
But how can anyone say that?
How can anyone believe it?
O.K., maybe for those who have died
   it is no more than a journey
   into a new world,
   into a new and wonderful life,
   where they are released from the disease,
   pain and evil of this world.

But what about those who are left?
What about family and friends
   who must go on to face life
   without loved ones?

It just seems that people
   have a lot to say
   about the experiences of those
   who have died, Lord,
   but knowing that people we love
   are happy and well
   is only half of the battle.
It seems like no one really wants to address
   the real issues, Lord.

You see, Lord,
    for those who are left,
    death *is* something.
Death is a lot of things.

Death is anger and bitterness
    at being deprived of a loved one,
    at being left to cope all alone.

Death is pain and hurt
    as people find a gaping hole
    in their lives.
A hole which can never be filled.

Death is regret and guilt
    about things that have been said and done,
    about things which haven't.

Death is a sense of injustice and waste,
    as it is realised that talents
    and aspirations
    will never
    be fulfilled.

Death is a confusion of these emotions.
Death is all of this and so much more.

So why is the subject evaded, Lord?
Why does no one have any answers?
Why can no one offer any real comfort?

I know it's because you are the only one
    with the answers.
You, Lord, are the only one
    who can ever truly comprehend death.
The only one
    who knows why it must happen.
The only one
    who knows what happens.

I know, Lord,
    that being mere mortals,
    our minds could never understand
    your infinite wisdom,
    but knowing this does not take away
      the grief.
It does not make it any easier
    to deal with, Lord.

So all I can do
    is ask for your help again, Lord.
As you are the only one
    who understands death,
    then surely you are the only one
    who can offer any comfort.

So, Lord,
I pray now for the ones who are left.
The ones who are hurting and lonely,
    the ones who are continually asking,
    'WHY?'

Lord, please help those
    who have lost loved ones.
Melt their angered and bitter hearts,
    ease their troubled and guilty minds.
Make people realise that in death
    there is a purpose, there is a justice.

Help people to untangle
    their confused emotions.
Help them to deal with their sorrow.

Above all, Lord,
    please help people to realise
    that they are not alone in their grief.
Help them to remember
    that you understand
    their pain and hurt,
    for you yourself had to watch
    as they put your own son to death
    on a cross.

Let people know that you share
    in their loss and sadness,
    and that, given the chance,
    you can offer them the comfort
    and hope they so longingly seek.

Thank you, Lord.

Amen.

FRIENDS: FRAGILE –
HANDLE WITH CARE

Lord,
   why doesn't each new friendship come
   carefully wrapped in bubble wrap, in a
   big cardboard box with care instructions
   and marked with the words,

   'Fragile – handle with care'?

Maybe then I would be a little more careful
   and treat my friends with the care and
   attention they deserve.
Maybe then more people would realise
   that friendship is precious and that
   precautions must be taken in order to
   preserve it.

You see, far too often
   friendships are neglected,
   communication breaks down,
   people are hurt,
   friends drift apart,
   and all for the sake of a phone call.
A letter.
A quick word.

Crazy, isn't it?

You know, Lord,
    the girl round the corner got married
    last weekend,
    or so I was told.
That girl was my best friend for eight years,
    we were inseparable.

Then I started going to church,
    I met new friends and found new interests.
O.K., Lord, so people change,
    grow older, move on.
It's all part of life's great design
    I suppose.
But the thing is
    that I never invited her along,
    I never introduced her to my new friends,
    I never tried to make our friendship last,
    I just abandoned it.
I know my life must be all the poorer for it.

And now I look at my current friendships,
    Lord, and I really must thank you,
    for I have some really great friends.
People who I know will always be there
    for me
    no matter what.
Sharing my ups and my downs,
    my successes and my failures,
    my tears and my laughter,
    my stresses,

my terrible jokes,
my life.

Where would I be without any of them, Lord?
Friends from college,
    from church,
    from school,
    from work.
Each of them so different,
    so unique,
    so special,
    so precious to me.

And yet, Lord,
    how often have I taken them for granted,
    not found the time to write or phone,
    or even to just tell them
    how much they mean to me
    and that I am there for them
    if they ever need me.
How many times have I abused a relationship?
How often have I spoken unkindly?
I cringe just to think about it, Lord.

So all I can do now, Lord,
    is pray for my friendships.
Pray that my friends might find it
    in their hearts to forgive me
    for being such a terrible friend.
Pray that they will realise that they do mean

the world to me even if I don't always
make it clear.

But pray especially, Lord,
    that you will help me
    to be a better friend.
To be more thoughtful,
    more caring,
    more understanding,
    more willing to make sacrifices
    and put myself out for my friends,
    so that, with your blessing,
    I may be able to enjoy their company
    for many more years to come.

Amen.

SAY A PRAYER

God, have you ever felt helpless?
    Useless?
Like you're in a position to do something,
    to help someone,
    but the right words,
    the right actions,
    they just never surface?
I guess not, Lord.
It's just that I sat there today, Lord,
    with my friend.
I could see my friend's hurt,
    I could feel my friend's despair,
    but there was nothing I could do
    to make things O.K.

I searched for the right words,
    for some earth-shattering statement
    that would make the hurt more bearable.
That would help resolve confused thoughts,
    but the hurt and the confusion remained.

So I reached out and hugged my friend,
    desperately wanting to hug
    all the tears away,
    wanting to help ease the pain.
But the tears and the pain remained.

There really was nothing I could do to help,
    even though I racked my brain
    over and over for a possibility.

So I told my friend that I was always there
    if I was needed.
I told my friend that I cared,
    yet even that did not seem enough.

Then as I left, I told my friend
    that I would say a prayer.

So now, Lord, I do just that.
I pray for my friend.
I ask you to ease my friend's pain and hurt,
    to guide my friend through the confusion,
    to wipe away my friend's tears,
    to make things O.K. again.

And all of a sudden, Lord,
    that seems like nearly enough.
All of a sudden,
    I don't feel quite so useless,
    quite so helpless.

Thank you, Lord, for helping me realise.

Amen.

TORN IN TWO

You know, Lord,
    I wish I could split myself
    in two,
    I wish I could clone myself or something,
    just so I can be
    in two places
    at the same time.

You see, Lord,
    I feel a bit
    like I live in two different worlds,
    like I live
    two completely different lives,
    almost like
    I'm two completely different people.

It's as if there's my home world
    with one set of family
    and friends,
    with one way of life.

Then there's my university world
    with a completely different
    set of friends,
    and a completely different
    way of life.

There are different routines,
    different people to consider,
    different places to haunt,
    differences in what is considered
    acceptable and what is not.

Even differences
    in what people talk about
    and are interested in.

Its not that either world
    is any better than the other,
    just that they're different.
The problem is, Lord,
    that sometimes I feel
    like there is no bridge between them,
    like I'm being torn in two.

Every time I leave one world
    I can't help feeling sad,
    but at the same time
    I am excited at going to the other one.
The problem is in choosing between them.
I mean, Lord,
    how can I possibly do that?

And yet there are often times
    when I must.
Times when there are events happening
    in both worlds,

like birthday parties
and other celebrations,
both of which I really want to go to.

Then comes the time when
I must choose between them.
It really is an impossible decision, Lord.

The really big problem
is knowing that one day
I will have to make the final decision
about which group of people
I want to stay with.

About which place I want to reside in.
About which world I want to live in.
What a nightmare, Lord!

So often in the past I have tried
to remedy the situation.
Tried to avoid making the decision
by mixing my two worlds,
by building little bridges between them.
But it can be so difficult, you know,
so awkward,
so unsuccessful.

Because, although I feel perfectly at home
in both of my worlds, it doesn't mean
that my friends and family will.

In fact, it sometimes seems
    that the contrary is true.

Sometimes it makes me feel so tense
    and uncomfortable
    that, well, I have to be honest, Lord,
    I usually try to avoid
    such situations now.

So all I can do is carry on,
    hoping that somehow
    I will be able to make both sides
    realise how much
    they mean to me,
    how much I want
    to be with them both,
    and how torn in two I feel.

I suppose what I am asking, Lord,
    is for you to make the decision for me.
I know it's a cop out,
    but what else can I do, Lord?
I really am not strong enough
to do it myself.

So please, Lord,
    make your will clear to me.
Let me know where I am supposed to be,
    who I am supposed to be with,
    and who I am supposed to be, full stop.

And whatever your will, Lord,
    please don't allow me
    to lose contact with either world,
    because even though they are so different,
    even though they make me feel torn in two,
    the truth is I want to be a part
    of both of them.

Please, Lord?

Amen.

CHANGE

Change!
You know, Lord,
    the word alone instils fear in me,
    stirring up all those insecurities
    and doubts that for so long
    have lain dormant.
And yet, the experience is even worse.

Right now, Lord,
    I feel like my life is being unravelled,
    like a tattered
    old jumper.

Many of my friends are moving away,
    my relationships with others are changing,
    I'm living in a new flat,
    I'm about to start a new job.
In fact, Lord,
    it feels like absolutely everything
    in my life is either different
    or new.

And even though I'm struggling desperately
    to hold everything together,
    to keep things as they are,
    I can feel the wool being pulled
    through my fingers.

And there is nothing I can do
    to hold onto it.

And now,
    almost nothing remains intact
    of the familiar and secure life
    that had fitted me like an old,
    favourite jumper;
    comfortable and worn.

And I feel such a sense of loss
    and sadness, Lord,
    as each stitch falls away.
Yet all I can do is watch helplessly
    as one by one I bid farewell
    to family
    and friends.
Feeling like the only certainty left
    is that nothing will ever be
    the same again.

And I am so full of regret, Lord.
There is so much I should have said,
    So much I should have done.
Now all I have left
    are missed opportunities,
    and a whole bunch of 'what ifs'.

How I wish I had appreciated my life
    and all it contained

before it was unwoven like this,
and changed beyond all recognition.

All I can do now is watch
cautiously and fearfully
as the unravelled thread is knitted
steadily into a new pattern.
Into a new life for me to live,
with a new home,
new relationships,
a new job.

I admit, Lord,
that the pattern unfolding before me
is bright and exciting.
But I am finding it so difficult
to see beyond the unfamiliarity
and uncertainty
that I must deal with.

This new life feels so much like
a new cotton shirt;
stiff and uncomfortable.
And I long for my old, favourite jumper,
my old friends,
my old home,
my family,
my old life.

Oh, Lord,

I know my protests are in vain,
I know everything must change,
I know all this is your will.
But why now, Lord?
Why do things always have to change
    when life is flowing along nicely?

I guess that I'll never know the reasons
    and so all I can do is turn to you, Lord.
All I can do is ask you to help me through,
    to help me remember that the pattern
    being woven,
        is being woven by you,
That it is your design for my life.

Please, Lord,
    guide me through each new stitch,
    each new relationship,
    each new experience.

Please, Lord,
    comfort me by reminding me
    that the old thread,
    my old relationships,
    have not been discarded.
    Only woven differently.

Please, Lord, forgive me
    for all I've done wrong in the past
    and help me to learn

from my 'dropped stitches'.
Most importantly, Lord,
    help me to realise
    that there is one thing that remains
    unchanged,
    unchanging,
    unchangeable,
    through all the patterns of my life.
That is your unending love for me, Lord.

Amen.

PARTY TIME! EXCELLENT!

Pubs!
I'm not ashamed to say it, Lord,
    I think pubs are great.
Being able to meet up with my friends,
    sharing a couple of drinks
    and a few laughs,
    catching up on all their latest news.

And as for clubs?
I love clubs.
All that time spent just deciding
    what I'm going to wear,
    then throwing away all my usual
    inhibitions,
    losing myself in the atmosphere and music,
    and dancing and singing the night away.

And parties?
I *really* love parties.
After all,
    I can have the best of both worlds here,
    what more could anyone ask for?

And festivals are good as well, Lord.
All that sitting out in the sunshine,
    listening to and watching my favourite
        bands,

feeling as though I could almost be
in a different world,
a relaxed, laid-back world,
a world where people actually get on
with each other.

And what about funfairs?
I think they're great as well, Lord.
Throwing on my old clothes and regressing
back to my childhood,
giggling and screaming,
desperately trying to scare myself
to death on all those rides.

And balls and weddings
are just brilliant too.
Getting dressed up in all those poncy clothes
and jewellery,
making believe, for one day,
that I am actually
elegant and sophisticated.
(Pretty hard to believe I know, Lord!)

I love all of these things, Lord,
All of life's events,
All of life's wonderful parties.

And the reasons I love them
are so simple, Lord.
I love them for all the opportunities
they give me.

Like the opportunity to have fun
    with my family and friends,
the opportunity to relax and escape
    from the hassles of the day,
the opportunity to let my hair down
    and just clown around.
Basically, Lord,
    the opportunity to really be myself.

I do realise, Lord,
    that partying is not always good.
I know people can go too far and ruin things.
And I do know that there is much more
    to life than partying.

But without it at all, Lord,
    I'm sure I wouldn't enjoy life
    nearly as much.
I'm sure I wouldn't have nearly
    as much fun.

So I just want to thank you for all
    the great partying
    that I've managed to do.
For all the good times I have shared
    with my family and friends.

And I pray that there may be many more
    parties to come in the future,
    because one thing is clear to me, Lord,

51

you have certainly given us
plenty to celebrate.

Thanks, Lord.

Amen.

*. . . I have come that you may have life,
and have it to the full.*

John 10:10

STRESS HEAD

Oh God,
    I really need you now,
    I mean more than I have ever
    needed you before.
    I know I say that every time, Lord.

I know I said all this just before my
    driving test.
I know I said it before my
    job interview.
I know I said it when I thought I wasn't
    going to be able to pay
    the gas bill.
I know I've said it before
    every first date
    I've ever had.
But this time
    I really REALLY mean it, Lord.

The thing is,
    I really cannot do this without you,
    and to be honest,
    I am not sure I can even do it with you.

I am just so stressed, Lord.
I mean REALLY stressed,
    like, my heart feels as though it's about

to burst out of my chest,
like, I'm sure I'm gonna be sick
any minute now,
like, there's absolutely no way that I'm
going to get any sleep tonight.

You see, Lord,
my first exam is tomorrow.

TOMORROW!
MY FIRST EXAM!

Can you believe it?
I've got so much work left to do,
so much left to learn,
so much left to memorise.
I'm sure that I'll never do it in time.

I just know that I am going
to let myself down,
that I am going to let my parents down,
that I am going to let you down.
And as for my friends?
My friends are going to think
I'm so stupid.

Do you know, Lord,
if I felt I could,
I really would jack all this in now,
just not bother turning up tomorrow,

but I know that would be stupid,
I know I've got to at least try.

The problem is, Lord,
    that no matter how much I try to reassure
    myself that it really does not matter how
    I do in these exams,
    no matter how many times people tell me
    that exams really are not that important
    when it comes into the grand scheme
    of things,
    I still know deep down that they are
    important.

That the grades I get from these will be the
    sum total of three years of my life,
    and that they will probably determine
    the rest of my life and what I will
    and will not be able to do with it.

I know it probably sounds to you, Lord, like
    I'm just being melodramatic,
    like I'm just being a stress head,
    as usual.
After all, stress head by name,
    stress head by nature.
That's me, God.
But these exams really are
    important to me.

Maybe that's the problem.
Maybe they're too important.

I just can't help feeling after my last set
     of terrible grades that I really have got
     something to prove.
Not just to my family
     and friends,
     but to myself.

Still, Lord, I know you've helped me through
every other stress attack in my life,
I'm sure you won't fail me now.

So all I ask
     is that you WILL help me again,
     please, Lord.

Just help me to feel your spirit within me,
     to feel your comforting arms around me,
     to hear your gentle voice reassuring me,
     to feel that inner peace
     that only you can give.

And to remember, Lord,
     that, whatever happens now,
     your will
     will be done.

Amen.

Be still and know that I am God;
I will be exalted among the nations,
I will be exalted in the earth.

Psalm 46:10

Do not be anxious about anything,
but in everything, by prayer and petition,
with thanksgiving, present your requests
to God. And the peace of God, which
transcends all understanding,
will guard your hearts and your
minds in Christ Jesus.

Philippians 4:6, 7

RUINED

Oh, I am so angry, Lord,
    I just cannot believe it.
I mean, just look at the mess,
    it's just totally ruined.

And this used to be such a lovely place
    to come and eat my lunch.
The water was crystal clear,
    the grass was luscious and green.
Small fish could be seen
    just below the surface of the pond,
    and sometimes, a coot or duck
    would meander through the reeds.

On warm days,
    children would paddle and play
    whilst their parents sat on the grass,
    eating ice cream and basking in the sun,
    welcoming the break from the rat race
    which lay only yards away.

And now?
Well, it's ruined isn't it?
Totally ruined.

The water is covered in thick,
    nasty-looking oil.

The grass is littered with rubbish
   and cigarette ends.
The fish and the ducks,
   just like the people,
   are all gone.

The thing is, Lord,
   that this scene before me
   is so typical of the world
   we live in today.
People just seem to go around
   ruining all the beautiful gifts
   that you have given us.

I mean, Lord,
   just look at what we are doing
   to the rainforests.
Every day, acres and acres
   of beautiful forest are destroyed
   and with it all the many species
   of animal and plant life
   that we have not yet
   even discovered.

In its place are built huge cattle ranches
   which can remain on the land just a couple
   of years before it all turns into desert.

So there we have it, Lord,
   we take something as fertile,

as interesting,
as spectacular as the rainforests
and turn it into desert.

Then, of course, all this contributes
to the greenhouse effect
which is ultimately going to lead
to the destruction of all the wonderful
gifts you have placed on this planet.

And of course, Lord,
this is just one way in which we
are ruining our world.

There's all the pollution
of the air and seas
by big business
and everyday consumer goods.

There's the mass slaughter
of rare species
just so people can eat their delicacies.

There's all the dam-building
in many poorer countries
which floods acres of farmland,
destroys native people's homes
and livelihoods,
just so that the rich élite,
living in the cities,

can have the electricity supply
they demand.

I could go on, Lord,
but I think I've made my point.

The thing is, Lord,
everyone knows the damage we are doing
and no one seems to care.
No one does anything about it.
I mean, Lord,
why are people so stupid?
Am I the only person on this entire planet
who you managed to bless
with intelligence?
I know I'm not,
so why does this destruction continue?

Well, to be honest,
I think I know why really.
It's because we are all so selfish.
We don't care about
what we are depriving
other people of.

We don't care
about the mess
that we are leaving
for future generations.

We don't care
    that we are ruining
    the earth.

Lord, I feel so angry
    and so helpless.
What can I do to change anything?

Lord, I don't mean to be a defeatist,
    but I am just one insignificant person,
    so who is going to listen to me?

And now it dawns on me, Lord.
You are listening to me, aren't you?
I mean, that's a pretty strong force
    to have on my side,
    and as you are always reminding me, Lord,
    by faith I can move mountains.

So I pray to you, Lord.

Please help people realise
    what they are doing
    to the beautiful planet
    you have given us.

Please let them see
    all the damage they are doing,
    and the consequences of their actions.

Please let them be filled
    with compassion
    and remorse.

Help them to change their ways,
    even if it's just to start thinking twice
    before they buy an aerosol spray
    or leaded petrol for their car,
    because in this way, Lord,
    maybe our world
    won't be quite so ruined.

Amen.

THE SPICE OF LIFE

I imagine a world, Lord.
A world where everyone looks the same.
A world where people are all the same height
    and size,
A world where people all have the same skin
    and hair colour.
Sounds pretty boring doesn't it, Lord?

But then I go even further, Lord.
I imagine a world where everyone speaks
    the same language,
    all in the same accent.
A world where everyone shares
    the same culture
    and eats the same foods.
A world where everyone has the same
    personality.
A world where everyone thinks
    the same thoughts and says
    the same things.
Now that sounds devastatingly boring,
    doesn't it?

Then I look around me, Lord,
    at the world you have created,
    the people you have created.
    at the assortment of shapes and sizes,

at the patchwork of colours and creeds,
at the great range of personalities,
at the vast array of cultures.

You have made each of us so different,
so individual,
right down to the marks on our fingertips.

And the reasons for all this diversity,
the reasons for this wonderful medley
of people,
seem so very clear to me, Lord.

It's because you wanted to create a world
where we could all be individuals,
where we could all be people
in our own right, with our own beauty,
with our own free will.

It's because you realised from the beginning
that variety was the spice of life.
You knew that without it,
your world would not be nearly
so interesting,
not nearly so intriguing,
not nearly so beautiful.

I am so grateful, Lord,
that you have made the world
the way it is.

That you have made people the way they are,
  with all their many differences.

And I take great pleasure, Lord,
  in sampling other people's cultures
  and foods,
  in trying to learn foreign languages,
  in meeting and getting to know
  different people,
  in simply looking around me at the jumble
  of different faces.

Lord,
  all I ask is that when ignorance and fear
  blind people to the truth,
  when prejudice and discrimination
  take over their minds,
  that they may realise,
  as I hope I have,
  that it is you, Lord,
  who has made all of us so very different,
  and yet, at the same time,
  has made all of us in your own image.

Lord,
  please just help all of us to realise
  that variety really is
  the spice of life.

Amen.

OH, WHEN THE SAINTS

Martin Luther King,
    Mother Theresa,
    Bishop Desmond Tutu,
    Mahatma Ghandi,
    Nelson Mandela,
    Bishop Trevor Huddleston,
    Aung San Suu Kyi.

The saints of our time,
    the ones who are going to be marching in.
Not all of them are Christians, Lord, I know,
    but the thing is, they have all stood up
    for what they believed in.

They have all fought for the rights
    and welfare
    of others.
They have all loved their neighbours,
    usually to the detriment of their own
    lives and wellbeing.

They have all worked tirelessly
    to free the oppressed,
    to feed the starving,
    to save the dying,
    to give strength to the weak,
    to give hope to the disillusioned.

And yet they have all been
    just one voice alone,
    shouting against the crowd,
    shouting against the powerful,
    but they have all been heard, Lord.
They have all made a huge difference
    to people's lives,
    to the world we live in.

So often, Lord,
    I look at the world around me
    and see so much that needs to be changed,
    so much that needs to be put right.
All the inequality,
    all the violations of people's
    civil rights,
all the poverty and violence.

And I really long to be able
    to make a difference.
I really long to be heard.

But resignedly I think to myself,
    'I am just one person,
    shouting against the wave
    of popular belief.
    What can I possibly do?
    What difference can I possibly make
    to one person's life,
    let alone many people's?'

Then I remember those people
   who have achieved this.
The sacrifices they have all made,
   the impact they had on the world.

I remember the man
   who had the biggest impact
   of all.

The man born in a stable to a poor family.
The man who two thousand years later
   still has global recognition,
   who still has an impact
   on many people's everyday lives.

God as a man.

I realise that through you, Lord,
   anything is possible.
I realise that if I am willing to stand up
   and be counted,
   if my faith is strong enough,
   then I can make a difference.
And even if I only make one person's life
   a little more bearable,
   even if I only make one person's life
   a little happier,
   then all the sacrifices
   would surely be worthwhile.

So I turn to you, God, and say,
    'I want to be among that number,
    I want to make a difference,
    I want you to use me as a window
    for the rest of the world
    to be able to see your love.
    Use me as you will, Lord.
    Send me to wherever you want me.
    Let your will be done.'

Then perhaps, Lord,
    I will be able to say to myself,
    'I stood up for what I believed in,
    I loved my neighbour,
    I stood for Christ,
    I was amongst that number.'

Amen.

SHADES OF GREY

You know, God,
   I used to have such clear views on things.
The world seemed
   so very black
   and white,
   this was right,
   that was wrong,
   simple as that, really.

A few years on,
   a few years older,
   a few years wiser?

Everything seems so different.
Try imagining
   a whole rainbow of grey shades.
Well that's how I see the world now, Lord,
   as complicated as that.

Some call it being more open-minded,
   others call it growing up.
I call it being confused.

You see, Lord,
   as time has gone on
   I have met new people,
   I have heard new points of view,

I have experienced new situations.
And so, my old beliefs
   have been challenged.
Not just by others,
   but also by myself.

And the problem is, Lord,
   I really don't know
   what I think about things any more.
I don't know what I believe.

Well, take the issue of illegal drugs
   for example.
I always used to think
   that they were the evil of society,
   that drug users were either
   the victims of that evil
   or the advocates of it.
And now?

Well, for starters
   I've discovered that cannabis
   has medicinal properties,
   that it can be used
   in the treatment of AIDS and arthritis
   and probably much more.

And for seconds
   I've come to even doubt the evils
   of its recreational use.

I mean, Lord,
    the side-effects of smoking dope
    are certainly no worse
    than the effects of drinking alcohol
    or smoking cigarettes.
And how many stories do we hear
    about a group of people
    smoking a few joints
    and then starting a fight?
None, basically!

So how come we live in a society
    where alcohol is acceptable
    and yet smoking cannabis isn't?
I'm not trying to argue on behalf of the
    cannabis lobby here, Lord,
    but it does make you think, doesn't it?

Then, Lord, there is the issue of
    homosexuality.
Well how can I have an opinion on something
that no one really understands?
I mean, no one really knows whether the
    so-called 'condition' is genetic
    or psychological
    or something else entirely.
Even to call it a condition seems insulting.

I mean, these people don't know why
    they feel

the way they do, they just do.
So how can it be fair to deprive them of a
    fulfilling relationship
    just because they don't fit the norm?

And then there's crime, Lord.
All those activities which break the laws
    of our society,
Everything from rape to petty theft,
    all branded under one title.

I always believed that criminals
    were bad people,
    that they deserved to be put behind bars,
    that they should be kept separate
    from the rest of society.

And yet, so often it appears that theft
    and robbery are carried out by people
    living in the throes of poverty,
By people who have been denied access
    to the jobs and income they need
    to support their families.

By people just trying to fight back
    against the more privileged sectors
    of society.
By people who have never been taught
    the difference
    between right and wrong.

And so many other crimes,
    violent and dreadful crimes,
    are carried out by the mentally ill.
People in need of medical care and attention
    but who instead have been left
    to fend for themselves,
    thrown out into the community.

I am not trying to say that crime
    is not wrong, Lord,
    just that, as with so many issues,
    I no longer see things
    in black and white.

And the list of issues goes on and on, Lord.
Everything from sex to abortion,
    all of which have taken on new,
    hidden depths of grey
    which have confused my views.

So, Lord,
    I am looking to you now
    for the guidance I need on these issues,
    in the knowledge that you are the only
    one who holds the key to understanding
    what really is right and wrong.

I ask you, Lord, to help me sort through all
    those different shades of grey,
    to help me form the correct opinions,

to help me make the right decisions,
so that, no matter how confusing
the world may sometimes appear,
no matter how many different shades
I must examine,
I may still manage to know the black
from the white,
the right from the wrong.
And so, with your help,
I may always do what is right.

Amen.

*I will instruct you and teach you in
the way you should go;
I will counsel you and watch over you.*

Psalm 32:8

SO MANY QUESTIONS

Abortion!
Lord, what do you think about abortion?
I wish you would tell me,
I wish I knew what to think.

My gut instinct cries out that it is wrong,
     that it could never be right.
After all, Lord, you have told us
     that killing is wrong.
And that's what abortion is, isn't it, Lord?
Killing?

In a perfect world the issue might be as easy
     as that to resolve.
The problem is, Lord, that we do not live
     in a perfect world.
Far from it in fact.
There seem to be so many considerations
     to complicate the issue,
     so many questions that need answering.

I mean, Lord, what about if a girl
     falls pregnant after being raped?
Is an abortion acceptable then?
Or what about if the mother is very young?
Or if the mother's life is endangered
     by the pregnancy?

Is it then all right to abort?

And what about the child?
What if the child is likely to be born
    with a serious physical or mental
    disability?
So many people seem to believe that if a
    person's quality of life is threatened then
    this alone is good enough reason
    to carry out an abortion.
After all, we do live in a world which is
    particularly unsympathetic to those who
    are weak or different in some major way,
    and disability does bring a great
    emotional and financial burden.

But then I can't help feeling, Lord,
    that we are all just 'Hitlers',
    trying to justify our quest
    to create a perfect race.

And anyway, who has the right to decide
    about what does and does not constitute
    a good quality of life?
Who has the right to decide
    who should and should not live?

And if we do begin to justify abortion
    on these grounds
    then how far could it go?

Could we start arguing that it is right
    for people with a below-average income
    to not follow through with a pregnancy
    just because the lack of money may result
    in a poor quality of life?
Could we start justifying the decision
    of some mothers to abort female foetuses
    just because they are a financial burden
    to the family,
    as opposed to males
    who are potential breadwinners?
Could we start saying that
    black and Asian babies should be aborted
    because they are likely to encounter
    racial harassment and discrimination?

I know this may be taking the argument
    to extremes, Lord,
    but I really do wonder.

Even if we do accept that under certain
    circumstances abortion may be the best
    option, then there is yet another set of
    questions for which we have no answers.

Like, up to what age is abortion acceptable?
When does life begin?
At what point can a baby be considered a
    person with a soul of its own?
At birth? At conception?

Somewhere in between?
In the Bible you tell us that you knew us
    even before we were born,
    so where does that leave us, Lord?

Lord, I really wish I had the answers.
So often I am asked my point of view,
    so often I would like to say that I think
    abortion is wrong,
    but there are so many
    complicating possibilities,
    So many unanswered questions.

And what if it was me, Lord?
What if I ever have to make the decision?
I like to think that I would never
    have an abortion,
    but to be honest, Lord,
    I even question this sometimes.

You see, Lord, I have so many plans,
    so many things I really want to do
    that I just would not be able to do
    if there was a baby on the scene.
Then I think about my situation,
    my low income that barely supports
    just me.
My irresponsible nature,
    my age,
    the possible reaction from my family
    and friends.

I have got to admit that I really can see
    the attraction of just being able
    to end the pregnancy
    without anyone else finding out.

I really do pray, Lord,
    that if it ever came to it,
    I would make the correct decision.
That I would realise
    that what I was dealing with was a life,
    a precious and God-given life.

Even more though, Lord, I pray that
    I will never have to make the decision.
That if I ever fall pregnant
    it will be under the best circumstances.

But, as I have said already, Lord,
    I realise that this world is far from perfect,
    and so, as ever, I turn my eyes to you.

You are the one with all the answers,
    all I have is questions.
All I ask is that you will give me
    just a bit of an idea,
    just a small clue,
    just so that I would know for once,
    a little of your will.

Amen.

THE JOY OF WOMANHOOD

Lord, Why?
Why was I so unfortunate
    to have been born a female?
It's not that I want to be a man, Lord,
    just that being a woman
    is sometimes so difficult,
    so frustrating,
    so annoying.

First of all, Lord,
    there is the pressure
    from society
    to be beautiful.

Every time I switch on the TV
    or turn the pages of a magazine
    I am confronted by images
    reminding me how I am supposed to look,
    or by advice columns
    telling me how to achieve
    this ideal.

I sometimes feel that my failure
    to achieve that beautiful face,
    that perfect complexion,
    that flowing hair,
    that model figure,

basically renders me
inadequate
as a person.

And I know that I'm not the only one
    who feels this pressure, Lord.
I only have to look around me,
    at a society where
    eating disorders abound,
    where cosmetics and beauty products
    are big business,
    where cosmetic surgery is becoming
    increasingly commonplace,
    just to know that my experience
    is the same as that of so many others.

Then there is the problem
    of sexual discrimination.
The facts speak for themselves here, Lord.
Women are over-represented in the low-status
    jobs which offer little security
    and pay less money,
    the jobs which offer few rights,
    the jobs with fewer opportunities.

And this is the case
    even in your own church, Lord.

So here I am now,
    just like many other women,

having worked like crazy
to do well at college.
Having done my best
in every job I have had,
only to be treated
like a brainless bimbo
by my male colleagues.
Only to find my future prospects
are not as bright as was promised.

I know that there are some professions
in which I can do well.
The so-called 'caring' professions.
Those jobs which fit in
with society's ideas of femininity.

Jobs like nursing,
or teaching,
or social work.

And it's not that these jobs
are not appealing,
it's not that I don't realise
their value in society.
It's just that I would like to have
the same choices that men have.

Of course, I do have some choice, Lord.
I mean, I could always be
a housewife, couldn't I?

I could stay at home every day
    and do the housework.
You know, Lord,
    the woman's domain;
    the washing
    and ironing
    and cleaning.

All those exciting jobs
    which are my birthright
    and duty whether I do choose to work
    or not.

Yes, Lord,
    it seems to me that my options
    are very clear.
Either I choose community service
    or I am sentenced to a life
    of domestic labour.
Not much of a choice is it, Lord?

And as if all this wasn't enough,
    there are still all those
    niggly little things.

The monthly mood swings
    and stomach ache.
People's expectations that I should want
    to get married and have children.
The sexist comments

and behaviour
that are intended to offend.

I really do think, Lord,
  that being a woman
  is really quite a burden to bear.

And yet, Lord,
  even though I grumble and complain and
  wish that things were different,
  the truth is that I can cope
  with all this.

All this is just part of life.
And I look at men and realise that they too
  have their burdens, that they too
  have their problems and battles.

There is just one thing, Lord,
  that I cannot cope with.
Just one thing that really grates;
  being told that I, as a woman,
  am inferior in your eyes, Lord.

Being told by certain churches that,
  because I am a woman,
  I can never minister to people,
  I can never lay my unclean and evil hands
  on the holy sacrament.
Do you know how that makes me feel, Lord?

Is it really true?

You know, it really hurts to believe
    that it might be.
To believe that simply because of my sex,
    I can only ever be a second-rate Christian.

I mean, it could be true couldn't it?
After all, what other reason could there be
    for you not to have any women
    amongst your apostles?

But I don't believe it is the case, Lord.
I really pray that I am right.
After all, you were born of a woman,
    you were born of the Virgin Mary.
And when you rose from the dead,
    the first person you revealed yourself to
        was not a man,
It was Mary Magdalen,
A woman.
I know, Lord, that whilst I live, I shall
    never know the truth about this issue,
    but I do pray, Lord, that whilst you help
    me to deal with all the other issues
    that I must face as a woman,
    that most of all you might help me
    with this one.

Amen.

THE MONSTER INSIDE

Out of control,
    that's what I am.
You see, Lord, there's this monster in my
    head.
It controls my feelings,
    dictates my thoughts,
    determines my actions.

The calorie counting,
    the bingeing,
    the vomiting,
    the exercising.

I know that if people found out
    they would think I was crazy,
That's why I barely admit to even myself
    that there is a problem.
You see I am not crazy,
    it all seems very rational to me.
Just an effective way of losing weight.
After all,
    it's a method I have used for years.

Only now I feel the monster growing stronger
    and stronger,
This obsession is taking over my life.
My every thought is consumed by it,

my emotions are ruled by it.
I am beyond the point of denial,
    totally out of control.

The yearning to lose weight
    is becoming so intense,
    the fear of gaining weight is so strong,
    that every time I look in the mirror
    I see through the monster's eyes.
Every time I eat anything
    the monster tells me not to,
    every time I dress
    the monster tells me to cover up well.
The only respite I get is when I sleep.
Some days I long for sleep,
    long to sleep forever.
Then I would be free.
But every morning I wake
    and the monster's claws
    are still firmly embedded.

Sometimes I wonder who is holding on
    more tightly;
    the monster or me.
You see, Lord, it should be easy.
I should just stop counting those calories,
    stop dieting,
    stop throwing up,
    but although life with my monster is hell,
    without it I would have nothing at all.

For too long now this monster,
    this obsession,
    has been my whole life.
Take it away and what do I have left?
What is there to strive for?
What do I think about?

I know deep down
    that life would be so much better
    but my fear of the unknown
    prevents me from finding out.

Stupid isn't it, Lord?

I have had help as well,
    people trying to help me
    exorcise the demon.
But all I do is tell them
    what they want to hear.
I know I shouldn't, but it's so much easier
    than having to deal with the issue,
    so much easier than having to deal
    with all my confused emotions.

So now, Lord,
    I turn to the one counsellor
    who can really help me;
    you, Lord.

I know I can't avoid the issues

with you, Lord,
    for you know my every thought.
I know you understand how I feel,
    even before I try to explain.
And I know you don't think that I am crazy.

Lord, I ask you now to help me
    to get rid of this monster in my head,
    I know it will be a long, painful process,
    and I'm not expecting instant results.

All I ask is that you will be my strength
    when I am weak,
    that you will give me confidence
    when I have none,
    that you will make me feel loved
    and valued and beautiful.

What I want most of all though, Lord,
    is for you to fill the gap that is left
    in my life when my obsession subsides.
To fill it with your love,
    to give me a new purpose,
    to help me take control
    of my thoughts,
    emotions and desires,
    so that I can once again
    enjoy being alive, being awake.

Amen.

FAIRY TALE ENDING

It's the theme of so many fairy tales,
    so many movies,
    so many novels.

Girl and boy meet,
    they eventually find a love strong enough
    to overcome all the odds, they live
    happily ever after,
    THE END.

So perfect and yet so simple.
So, Lord,
    where is my happy ever after?
Where is my fairy tale?
Where is the dashingly handsome prince
    who will stride into my life,
    woo me,
    fight tirelessly to win my love,
    and then whisk me away
    in one final romantic scene?
Basically, Lord,
    where is my 'Mr. Right'?

It sometimes feels that the harder I look,
    the further away he becomes.
And in his place?
Plenty of Mr. Wrongs.

Everyone from Mr. Tooserioustoosoon
    to Mr. Notatallinterested,
    Mr. Clingy to Mr. Heartless,
    Mr. Trouble to Mr. Boring.

And the list goes on,
    as does the heartache,
    the tears,
    the loneliness,
    the guilt.

I just want someone to love me, Lord,
    the same way I love them.
Is it so much to ask?

Just someone who I can trust,
    someone who will put me first,
    someone who's always there for me
    when I need him.
Someone to hold,
    someone I can share my life with.
I just want my happy ending, Lord,
    that's all.

I know this is real life
    and that happy endings
    don't just happen.
I know they have to be worked at,
    but I would appreciate
    just having the opportunity to try, Lord.

Oh Lord,
    I know I'm still young,
    but it feels like everyone else
    has someone special,
    and me?
Just lots of Mr. Wrongs
    and heartache
    and no happy ending in sight.

Lord,
    I know there must be a fairy tale for me
    somewhere out there,
I know I have to be patient.
I know that there is plenty of time for me,
    but just don't let it take too long,
    please, Lord.

Amen.

MEN

God created man,
   stood back,
   took a long hard look
   at what he had created,
   thought, 'I can do better than that',
   then created woman.

No, but seriously, Lord,
   Men.
They are a very strange species you know.
So different from women.

I mean, take a look at how they deal with
   emotion for example,
   or rather, how they avoid
   dealing with emotion.

Anyone would think that the words
   'I love you'
   were a foreign language to men.
One that they find
   particularly difficult to master.
And the only time they ever tell their mates
   how they feel about them is
   when they've had a few pints,
   then suddenly everyone
   is their best friend ever.

And as for crying?
Oh well, strictly taboo,
    unless they're in
    female company of course,
    then they might just manage
    a sniffle or two.

And why do men always have to be
    so rational
    about everything?
Why is there always a perfectly good
    explanation for everything?
And why are they so unromantic?

And what about their fascination
    with driving like a crazy person.
Is there some secret competition
    that I don't know about
    where the winner is the one
    who can most outstandingly
    break the speed limit,
    whilst taking a very tight bend,
    and bopping along
    to a very loud stereo?

And men can be such
    thoughtless creatures as well, Lord.
They really seem to have got
    'saying the wrong thing at the wrong time'
    down to a fine art.

And what about their incredible ability
　　to forget things?
They just never seem to realise
　　the importance of birthdays
　　and anniversaries,
　　unless it's their own, of course.

I know all this is pretty stereotypical,
　　and it's all said tongue-in-cheek
　　of course,
　　but sometimes men really do seem
　　so very different from women.

That's not to say that women
　　are perfect, of course.
I know better than anyone
　　how irrational we can be.
How catty we can be.
How soppy and over-emotional we are.
How good we are at remembering
　　everything and then holding it against
　　people for as long as we possibly can.

I know that men must find us
　　a pretty strange species
　　as well, Lord.

So why are we meant to go together, Lord?
Why do we even choose to?
Is it just the challenge

of trying to work each other out?
Of trying to discover what goes on
   in each other's heads?

Or is it that we were made
   to complement each other?
To draw the best out of each other
   and ourselves?

I can't help thinking
   that it's a bit of both, Lord.
And I've got to say,
   that's the way I like it.
You see, men are a strange species.
They really can be quite bizarre.
But if they weren't?
Then I'm sure life wouldn't be nearly
   so interesting,
   it wouldn't be nearly
   so much fun.

So, thank you, Lord,
   for men,
   thank you for making them
   so strange,
   for making us all
   so different.

Amen.

HERE I AM AGAIN

Oh, God,
    I just can't believe it.
Here I am again, Lord,
    on my knees, crying,
    completely brokenhearted,
    begging for your help.

I was so sure I had finished
    with all of this.
I mean, I'd completely given up
    on this love thing.
When I met him
    my heart had just been broken
    so badly I thought it was never
    going to mend.
I felt like I was at the lowest point
    of my life.
I felt so insecure,
    so worthless.
I had no self-confidence,
    no faith in relationships.

I cried out to you, Lord,
    just as I am now,
    but it felt like my prayers
    were a long time in being answered.
I began to think that even you

weren't listening,
that even you didn't care.

But then along he came,
the answer to my prayers.
With his arms open wide,
his caring words, his promises, his love.
He helped me put back the pieces of my life,
to restore my faith,
to build my self-esteem.

I felt special and cared for.
I felt safe and secure.

But still I held back, Lord,
scared of getting involved again,
scared of this.
I denied my feelings for him time after time,
fighting against the instincts
of my heart.
But eventually, I just had to give in.
The thing was,
I loved him.

So I lowered the barriers
and allowed him to see the real me.
I trusted him with my feelings,
with my heart,
with my love.
Oh, why, God?

WHY?

Just as before, my trust was betrayed.
The arms that once held me close,
    pushed me away, rejected me,
    cast me aside like a piece of litter.
And now I am hurting so much inside,
    I feel like I could die.

My heart is so bitter,
    my mind so confused.
I doubt his every motive,
    question his every intention.

All I can do now is pray to you, my Lord.
Ask you to ease my hurt,
    dry my tears,
    melt my bitterness.
Please, Lord,
    help me to pull the pieces of my life
    back into place and carry on.
Give me the strength I need to forgive him,
    the wisdom I need to let go of him,
    and the faith I need to love again,
    because one thing is for sure,
    I am here again,
    and this won't be the last time.

Amen.

SO VERY SORRY

Oh, God,
    this must be the worst feeling in the world.
Worse than being finished with,
    worse than being rejected,
    worse than anything.

It's the guilt I can't cope with.
I just can't bear the thought
    of what I've done,
    and the hurt I've caused.

All I could do was sit and watch
    as the tears welled up in his eyes,
    as his heart was breaking.
I really wanted to reach out and hold him,
    to say how sorry I was,
    to say that I still wanted to be friends,
    to say that I still cared.

But he just pushed me away,
    and I can't blame him really.
The closest I came to comforting words
    were just corny clichés.
The thing is though, Lord, I meant them.

And now I feel so guilty,
    so sad, so confused.

Guilty because of all the upset
    I've caused him.
Guilty because I know how he's feeling
    right now.
I've been there myself, Lord,
    and I know how much it hurts,
    and I know that I am the one
    who is causing that hurt.

Sad because someone close,
    a whole way of life,
    has been lost,
    gone forever.

Confused because,
    well, at first I was so sure
    that it was the right thing to do,
    the only thing to do.
My feelings had changed,
    I knew I had to end it,
    I couldn't lead him on.
But now?

Well, what if I made a mistake, Lord?
What if a couple of months down the line
    I realise that I do love him?
What if he was the one for me?
What if I phone him now
    and tell him that I want him back?
I mean just think how happy he'd be.

But I know I shouldn't.
I know it's better if I leave it.
I know it's all for the best.

Lord, I just pray
    that I've made the right decision.
I pray that you forgive me
    for the pain I've caused.
I pray that I'll never ever
    have to do this again.

Most of all, Lord, I pray for him.
Please help him to get over this,
    to get over me.
Help him to forgive me for what I've done,
    and make him realise
    that I never wanted this to happen.
That I really never wanted to hurt him,
    but that I just couldn't lie either, Lord.

I pray that one day he finds someone
    who feels the same way as he does.
Someone who will take good care of him,
    someone who will never hurt him.
A love that will last.

But for now, Lord, just let him know
    that I really am so very sorry.

Amen.

FORBIDDEN FRUIT

The forbidden fruit,
   there it sits, Lord,
   just slightly out of arm's reach.
It looks so tempting,
   so inviting.
If I were just to edge a little closer,
   just to get a better look,
   and maybe, have a little taste?

I don't know, Lord,
   perhaps I shouldn't.
After all, you have forbidden it.
So why is it
   that it looks so much more tasty
   than the other fruits around me?
Why is it so much more interesting?
Why is it so much more intriguing?
Why can't I just take a bite?
Would it really be so wrong?

I mean, it doesn't seem very fair, Lord.
Everyone else around me
   seems to have had a taste,
Everyone else is talking
   about how good it is,
   how much better it is
   than anything else.

All the magazines talk about it,
    people on television joke about it,
    books are even written about how tasting
    it can be made even better.

And it's not as if it's always
    out of reach either, Lord.
So often it is so close, and yet . . .
    so far.
So why, just because I am a Christian,
    must I say no?
Why can't I just have one small try?
It really is difficult sometimes, you know.

Everyone is pressuring me to try it,
    friends,
    boys,
    and that's not the worst of it.
There's all those raging hormones,
    all that thinking that I'm in love.
I mean, do you realise
    how difficult it is, Lord?
For people of my generation,
    in a society with permissive attitudes,
    to say no to sex?

And what is the point, Lord?
Why does it have to be like this?
Is it just to test our faith,
    or to make life difficult?

Or is it because the fruit tastes
   so much better
   after marriage?
Is it because it's such a special gift
   and you don't want it abused?

I suppose I'll never really know the answers.
All I do know, Lord,
   is that the fruit is forbidden
   for some reason,
   and I'm sure it looks all the sweeter
   because it is.

Amen.

MARRIAGE AND COMMITMENT

Lord,
   there is something really preying
   on my mind and I really need to talk
   to you about it.

It's about marriage and commitment.
Sounds heavy I know, Lord,
   it's just that, well,
   I find the idea of it, kind of, well,
   SCARY!
And to be honest with you
   I don't even know why, exactly.

I mean, it could be the idea
   of being committed to the same person
   for the rest of my life,
   of never again feeling that
   thrill of the chase,
   because if I ever get round
   to saying those vows, Lord,
   then I really do intend to keep them.

And how is anyone ever completely sure that
   they are with the right person?
After all, Lord, I am particularly good
   at getting things wrong, aren't I?

Or it could be the idea
    of losing my own identity,
    of ceasing to be a person
    in my own right,
    with my own beliefs,
    opinions and achievements,
    of just becoming part of a couple.

Then again,
    it could just be the thought
    of everything that goes hand in hand
    with being married.
You know, Lord,
    the mortgage,
    the kids,
    the responsibility,
    the growing up,
    the settling down.

Or it could be
    that I am just worried
    about how other people will see me,
Just worried that my relationships
    with my friends and family
    will change.

And yet again,
    it could just be the fact that
    so many marriages
    end in divorce these days.

The fear that this might be
 yet another thing
 I manage to fail at.

It could be a mixture of all of these, Lord,
 and the truth is,
 I just don't know.

I mean, I do like the idea of marriage.
The idea of being with the person you love
 until 'death us do part'.
The idea of being able to face life
 as part of a team,
 knowing that there is always
 someone there for me.

But for some reason,
 there is something about it
 that just makes me panic,
 just makes me want to run and hide.

Am I just scared of being happy?
Is there anyone else who feels like this?
Am I the only one?
Or does everyone go through this
 at some time in their lives?

I wish I knew all the answers, Lord.
I wish I knew why I am so scared,
 then maybe I could at least try

to sort it out in my head.
But all I can do is ask for your guidance
    on this one, Lord.
Ask you to ensure
    that I marry the right person.
Ask you to take away my fear.
Ask you to help me work hard at my
    relationship, so that it won't fail.
Ask you to help me realise that marriage
    is not something to be scared of,
        but that it's a wonderful gift from you.

If only I would really believe that, Lord,
then maybe I wouldn't be so scared.

Amen.

LOVE IS . . .

Love is . . .
   being myself, Lord,
   sitting around in my old clothes,
   without any make-up on,
   knowing that I'm still found attractive.

Love is . . .
   being able to say what's on my mind,
   giving my point of view,
   saying exactly what I think,
   knowing that, although not always
      agreed with,
   I am always respected.

Love is . . .
   being able to laugh,
   at life's many little mishaps,
   at all the mistakes I make,
   knowing that the joke is shared.

Love is . . .
   being able to share everything I have,
   everything I own,
   everything I am,
   knowing that my giving
   will be reciprocated.

Love is . . .
     being able to kiss and make up,
     after all those disagreements,
     after all the shouting and screaming,
     knowing that no grudges will be held.

Love is . . .
     all this and so much more.
It is a gift from you,
     a truly beautiful gift.

And yet, Lord,
     it has taken me so long
     to realise this.
I mean, Lord,
     I always thought of it
     as more of a burden really.
You know, one of those little tests
     you send us, Lord.

When I think of all those
     past relationships,
     all that time spent worrying
     about what I looked like,
     worrying about things that I said,
     scared to say what was really on my mind.

And all those grudges I held,
     all the barriers I put up
     to protect myself.

All the games I played.
All the insecurity and anger.
I really thought that all that
    was just part of love.
I really didn't understand what was meant
    about love being gentle and kind,
    but now, Lord?

I think I've found out what love really is.
I've found out that it really is
    gentle and kind.
Now I know that it truly is
    a gift from you.

Of course I realise that it does not
    always run smoothly.
I realise that it still has its ups
    and downs,
    that love needs to be worked at.

But, Lord, I also realise
    that love can win through,
That it can work
    without playing games
    and holding grudges.

So, Lord,
    I just want to thank you
    for the wonderful gift
    you have given me.

And I am so sorry
   that I ever doubted it.

Thank you, Lord,
for the love that I have.

Amen.

LOST IN THE DARK

I remember so clearly, Lord,
    that final flame fading away.
The embers glowing momentarily
    and then dying.
The lights going out on the maze
    which is my life.

And now here I am,
    alone!
The blackness enshrouding me
    like a huge velvet cloak,
    the silence echoing in my ears.

I shuffle forwards cautiously,
    arms nervously outstretched,
    reaching desperately into the corridors
    of my darkness,
    the caverns of my loneliness,
    searching for a flicker of hope,
    a guiding light,
    a friendly voice.

But there is no sound,
    there is no light.
Just dead end after dead end.
The walls drawing in on me
    and then moving away again.

I stumble and clamber and fall.
I am so confused,
   so scared,
   so bewildered,
   so tired.

All my effort is concentrated
   on overcoming each obstacle,
   on negotiating each turn in the path.
Life no longer has any aim,
   any meaning,
   any point.

Disorientated and disillusioned,
   I fall to the floor,
   and lying there in my silent tomb
   I start to wonder:
   wonder why you left me alone,
   wonder how I managed to drift
   so far away from the light,
   the warmth,
   the love,
   my Lord.

And now,
   my cries are splintering the silence
   like sheet glass.

   'Oh, where are you, Lord?
   Please don't leave me here alone.

Please come back to me
and help me see again.
Let me feel you close to me,
your spirit within me.
Let me see your guiding light ahead of me.
Please, Lord,
come back into my life.'

Then I hear your voice in my head,
calm and clear,

'Open your eyes and see me,
for I never left you.
I have always been here,
you just chose not to see.'

Realisation dawns in my confused mind
and I do your bidding.
The light floods into my life
like a river bursting its banks.
I feel your warmth, your love,
your spirit within me.

The maze still remains ahead,
winding, complicated
and confusing.
But now I see the route I must take,
and the choices I should make.
I see more clearly the obstacles
that lie ahead,

and I see how to overcome them.
My fear is beginning to subside,
    my life is filled with a new hope,
    a new joy,
    a new sense of meaning
    and purpose.

I have known the emptiness of going it alone,
    of closing my eyes to you.
I know now, Lord,
    that I am nothing without you,
    life is nothing without you.
You are my truth,
    my light,
    my way.

So hold me close now please, Lord.
Never let me turn my eyes away
    from you again.
I want you to be forever in my life
    and my heart.

Forever my Lord,
    forever my light.

Amen.

I love the Lord, for he heard my voice;
he heard my cry for mercy.
Because he turned his ear to me,
I will call on him as long as I live.

The cords of death entangled me,
the anguish of the grave came upon me;
I was overcome by trouble and sorrow.
Then I called on the name of the Lord:
'O Lord, save me!'

The Lord is gracious and righteous;
our God is full of compassion.
The Lord protects the simple-hearted;
when I was in great need, he saved me.

Be at rest once more, O my soul,
for the Lord has been good to you.

For you, O Lord, have delivered my soul
from death,
my eyes from tears,
my feet from stumbling,
that I may walk with the Lord in the land
of the living.

Psalm 116:1-9

WAYHEY!

Wayhey!
I'm so happy,
So very, very happy.
I feel like I could dance down the street,
    like I could sing in the rain,
    like I could climb a tree
    and shout my elation
    from its highest branches.

For once it really feels
    like absolutely everything
    is going right.
Like nothing now could possibly go wrong.
And it's all thanks to you, Lord,
    I realise that.

Even all the bad things I've had to face
    over the past few years suddenly seem
    to have a purpose,
Suddenly I realise why so many things
    have happened and that it has all
    just been a part of your huge plan.

Take my disastrous A-level results.
Well, if it hadn't been for those
    I would never have worked so hard
    for my degree.

I would never have got such a good grade,
    and I would never have got so much
    out of it.

And then take my last relationship.
If that hadn't been so heartbreaking
    I would never have appreciated
    the relationship I have now.
I would never have realised
    what a good thing I've got going here.

And the list goes on and on, Lord,
    and I know during the bad times
    I would have cried out to you
    in hurt and anger
    and frustration.
I know I would have been shouting
    and crying
    and wanting to know why these things
    were happening.

But now it all seems so clear
    and all I can do is say that I am sorry
    for ever doubting you
    and thank you for all I have now.
It really does not seem enough,
    but I really do mean it.

And so, Lord,
    I thank you for my family,

for all their love,
    support and friendship.
I thank you for my boyfriend
    and all he puts up with.
I thank you for all my wonderful friends.
I thank you for all the people
    in your church.
I thank you for all I have achieved
    over the last year.
And I thank you for all the opportunities
    you have offered for the years to come.

I feel like my life is so full and exciting
    at the moment and it's all down to you.
It's all down to the many gifts
    you have given me,
    the many prayers you have answered
        for me,
    the mountain of love you have offered me.

And all I can do now
    to express how I feel
    is to shout,

Wahey!
I love you, Lord – thank you !

Amen.

I will exalt you, O Lord,
for you lifted me out of the depths . . .

You turned my wailing into dancing;
you removed my sackcloth and clothed me
with joy,
that my heart may sing to you and
not be silent.

O Lord my God, I will give you thanks
for ever.

Psalm 30:1, 11-12

THE SPRINGTIME AFTER
THE WINTER

Desolate,
   bleak,
   dismal,
   joyless.
The dark, merciless skies loom
   above the forsaken earth.
Above the skeletal casualties of winter,
   stripped of their leaves and fruit.
Above the barren and chilling ground,
   stripped of its colour and vitality.
There are no signs of life.
No signs of hope.

And yet, Lord, my eyes appear to deceive me,
   for the earth is not dead, only sleeping.
Hibernating beneath its soft, white blanket.

And as the days grow longer,
   the earth eventually begins to stir,
   slowly waking from its deep
   and restful slumber.

Then gradually, the soft white blanket
   is folded back,
   the dark, grey skies are melted
   into shades of blue,

the cold, chilling bite of the air
is softened by the beaming, yellow sun,
and the cobwebs and rust are washed away
by the cool, refreshing showers.

And there, revealed,
	are the first green shoots,
	the first blossoms,
	the first signs of life awakening,
	the first signs of hope.

And now it seems there is no turning back.
Spring gains its own momentum,
	as reserves of pent-up energy and life
	explode into a vast mosaic
	of colour and activity.
Trees once more display their bright
	and cheerful robes.
The once-desolate ground is now carpeted
	in luscious shades of green.
In the fields, ice-white lambs jump and play
	under the watchful eye of their mothers,
	whilst on the pond, small fluffy ducklings
	take their first swimming lessons.
Spring has indeed arrived,
	in all its splendour and glory.

And yet, Lord, Spring seems to represent
	so much more than just the changing
	of the seasons.

You see, I remember
    another desolate scene,
    bleak,
    dismal,
    joyless.

I remember a man on a cross,
    stripped of his garments,
    stripped of his life.

I remember the followers of that man,
    their loss of hope,
    their devastation.

And I remember an empty tomb,
    a wondrous and glorious rebirth,
    an exciting new hope.

Lord,
    I really want to thank you for Spring,
    for all its colour and vitality,
    for all the hope it brings
    for the year ahead.

But I want to thank you even more for that
    most wonderful event that happened
    in the Spring, almost two thousand
    years ago.
I want to thank you for the crucifixion,
    for the sacrifices you made for me,

for the pain you bore for me,
all because your love for me was so great.

And I want to thank you
for the resurrection, Lord,
for the hope you have given me,
for the new life you have offered me,
for the Springtime after the Winter.

Thank you, Lord.

Amen.